MEDITATIONS
FOR THOSE OF MIDDLE YEARS AND MORE

By the same author:

Springboard for Easter (Mowbray) 1966
Meditation Outlines (S.P.C.K.) 1967
Holy Communion Manual (1967 Service), (Mowbray) 1967
Advent Candles (Mowbray) 1968
Layman's Lent (Mowbray) 1969
Experiment in Retreats (Mowbray) 1970
Prayers for Today (Mowbray) 1972
Abba Imma – a miscellany of pieces for the Parish Magazine (Canterbury Press Norwich) 1995
Making Marriage Work (Canterbury Press Norwich) 1996

Meditations for Lent
for those of
Middle Years and More

NORMAN W. GOODACRE

The Canterbury Press
Norwich

© Norman W. Goodacre 1996

First published 1996 by The Canterbury Press Norwich
(a publishing imprint of Hymns Ancient & Modern Limited,
a registered charity)
St Mary's Works, St Mary's Plain,
Norwich, Norfolk, NR3 3BH

British Library Cataloguing in Publication Data

A catalogue record for this book is available
from the British Library

ISBN 1-85311-150-3

*Typeset, printed and bound in Great Britain by
The Lavenham Press Ltd,
Lavenham, Suffolk*

Dedicated with gratitude and appreciation
to my parents,
Frank and Gertrude Goodacre.

FOREWORD

There was a bishop who said in his retirement that as he grew older he believed more and more firmly in less and less. The provocative remark was worthy of Bishop David Jenkins. For this reason spiritual counsellors often advise us to shed much and concentrate on a few resounding certainties to nourish the soul.

This collection of meditations is more subtle and to my mind more encouragingly helpful. They are composed by someone who has had years of experience as a spiritual director. He does not ask us to disown traditional ways but rather to translate them more imaginatively for our later years.

'We need to develop our sense of humour as we grow older'. That is a profound and not a trivial remark. People without a sense of humour lack a sense of proportion. Our Lord said to some upright defenders of religious rectitude 'You remind me of the children's song "We piped for you and you would not dance, we lamented and you would not mourn".' How to handle the laughter and tears of our humanity in later life is a major purpose of this book. It is not abstract. It is set against the landscape of Liverpoool with its buses and sea front. The frustrations of advancing years are gently woven into the text and illustrations culled from familiar moments of personalities in television or literature.

Wordsworth's 'Daffodils' can lead you through a city park, touch off a prayer for cancer sufferers and find you reflecting on the meaning of the word 'joy' in the scriptures. That is what seems to me to join together the lighter and more homely reflections with the solemnity that gathers round the sacred days of Good Friday and Easter. No laughter in the sanctuary of faith. No soft or glib phrases on the ultimate tragedies or the securities beyond.

There is a terse sentence in the farewell discourses of Our Lord which is well translated 'No one shall rob you of your joy'. That promise would make a fitting title for these evocative meditations.

The Rt Revd Lord Runcie

CONTENTS

ACKNOWLEDGEMENTS

The author and publisher are grateful to Methuen for permission to reproduce extracts from *Mind of the Maker* by Dorothy L. Sayers.

Material from *The Alternative Service Book 1980*, is copyright © The Central Board of Finance of the Church of England and is reproduced with permission.

Scripture quotations used for the meditations are from the Revised English Bible (REB) © Oxford University and Cambridge University Presses 1989 and reproduced with permission. Other scripture quotations used at opening of each section are adapted from the Authorized Version of the Bible.

INTRODUCTION

People live longer, retire earlier, and continue with work and study well into the fifties today. How does the traditional approach to Lent fare under these circumstances?

This study is an attempt to discover the immense possibility of a more mature approach to Lent for the older church person. Lent is traditionally a period of training and growth. It can, however, seem lengthy and tedious as we get older. This collection of readings is an attempt to cope with this situation: the pieces are short and subjects 'worldly' as well as 'churchy'. Facing the contemporary world and using it well is an essential ingredient in keeping a good Lent. We need to develop our sense of humour as we grow older, and cultivate a relaxed attitude to the heavily moral and critical spirit of today.

I have used the traditional pattern of Lent, laying the stronger emphasis on discipline during the last two weeks – Passion Week and Holy Week, when the Christian Church should be ready to follow Jesus to the Cross and beyond.

The object of the exercise, as St Paul makes clear, is to live life fully and freely to the glory of God, and to enjoy him for ever.

N.W.G.

FIRST FOUR DAYS OF LENT

ASH WEDNESDAY

The sacrifices of God are a broken spirit: a broken and
a contrite heart, O God, you will not despise.

Psalm 51.17

COLLECT
Almighty and everlasting God,
you hate nothing that you have made
and forgive the sins of all those who are penitent.
Create and make in us new and contrite hearts,
that, lamenting our sins
    and acknowledging our wretchedness,
we may receive from you, the God of all mercy,
perfect forgiveness and peace;
through Jesus Christ our Lord.

FIRST DAY OF LENT   *New Beginning*

There is always an opportunity for a new start. Life is full of new beginnings: it is never too late. When someone dies those of us who are left behind have to make a new beginning if we are to avoid self-pity. We need a goal. Advent looks towards Christmas and Lent towards Easter. We need a plan for a 'good' Lent.

Can this kind of 'new beginning' be achieved in 'the older years'? Have we not completed the main part of our life and work? We tend to think that we have seen it all before. The enthusiastic promoter of this 'mission' or that 'effort' does not find in us a keen response. But suppose we select something to offer that costs effort and at the same time appeals to our interest. There are always new approaches to Lent for a keen Christian. We can pray more reflectively and make spaces of quiet. We can maintain Sunday worship without a break for six weeks: receiving Holy Communion each Sunday and hearing the Word. You could step up your reading, choosing something quite different from the daily paper and the popular novel. There are a lot of simple religious books that you have never looked at and certainly never purchased. This is the moment to repair that omission.

There are Bible study notes available from the Bible Reading Fellowship, Sandy Lane West, Oxford OX4 5HG. Write for these and use them daily. Ash Wednesday is a good day to make this new beginning. Aim to study some aspect of the Christian faith that challenges you. Go back to school and by your own effort be your own teacher under God the Holy Spirit.

The Apostolic Spirit

Persevere in prayer, with minds alert and with thankful hearts; and include us in your prayers, asking God to provide an opening for the gospel, that we may proclaim the secret of Christ, for which indeed I am in prison. Pray that I may make the secret plain, as it is my duty to do. Paul in his letter to the Colossians 4. 2–4

SECOND DAY OF LENT *Joy*

'Have a joyful Lent.' Those words were spoken to Gillian Crow, diocesan secretary of the Russian Orthodox Church in Great Britain. In an article in *The Times* for March 4th 1995 she wrote: 'Lent is a letting go of worldly impedimenta leaving us free to take up our cross and follow Christ. His invitation was a dedication unto death, but a death bursting with new life at the core of each of us so that we can learn to shine with the glory of the Holy Spirit. It is to be filled with the great joy of the apostles at the Ascension, as they returned to Jerusalem to begin their new lives as Christ's body on earth.'

Lent lasts for six weeks; Ramadan, the Islamic fast, for one month – dawn to dusk each day. Taken seriously these fasts can be severe and testing and result in a much improved spiritual life. I have often thought that the Christian would do well to divide Lent into two sections: the first four weeks when special prayer and study can be undertaken, and the last two weeks – Passion Week and Holy Week – when a definite fast can be planned by limiting food and drink, sex and entertainment combined with continuing prayer and study.

In the older years physical disciplines are less easy though they can still apply and become effective offerings to God. The cheerful acceptance of disabilities, slowness of speech and grasp of what is going on – all make up a Lent which is most acceptable to God. Make your Lent a season of joyful acceptance of life as it is, and let it be filled with praise.

MEDITATION   **Blessed be God**

And when Elizabeth heard Mary's greeting, the baby stirred in her womb. Then Elizabeth was filled with the Holy Spirit and exclaimed in a loud voice, 'God's blessing is on you above all women, and his blessing is on the fruit of your womb.' Luke 1. 41

THIRD DAY OF LENT   *Choice*

One of the basics of the spiritual life is the ability to make right choices. Not only between right and wrong, but between wisdom and foolishness, courage and despair, obedience and going our own way. Choices are never easy when life is at its peak: as seniors we are often tempted to opt out altogether or sit on the fence. We face choices about where to live, about what amount of voluntary work we should do and about how to use available time and money well.

Various philosophies influence contemporary thinking and they affect personal choice. They can be summed up under three heads: politics, morals and science. Politics can suggest that life is controlled by economic forces outside ourselves; morality that we choose our behaviour because it is 'the way we are made'; science that life is determined by a kind of computer plan. Since each of these philosophies contains elements of truth for us we need a strong input of religious faith to assist in making the correct choice.

Directions for the Christian are to be found in Church and Bible. In the Book of Joshua for example we read: 'Choose this day whom you will serve; as for me and my people we shall serve the Lord.' Joshua 24. 15. This triumphant statement of faith in God can be paralleled in the New Testament when Jesus says to Peter and Andrew: 'Follow me and I will make you fishers of men.' Matthew 4. 19. We are free to choose and our life in the Church will make it possible to choose rightly. Following God's will should not be a spiritual contortion but made after consultation, prayer, and common sense and then offered to God who can set it aside if it is wrong.

MEDITATION
Jesus' prayer for his disciples

'Righteous Father, although the world does not know you, I know you, and they know that you sent me. I made your name known to them, and will make it known, so that the love you had for me may be in them, and I in them.

John 17. 25–26

FOURTH DAY OF LENT   *Confrontation*

Life is always challenging especially in the sphere of confrontation. We are angered over something and we want to fight. We see a crying need and would like to take action about it. Confrontation always includes self-confrontation as Henri Nouwen says in *Compassion*. We have to come to terms with our own aggression and violence. He quotes a piece by Thomas Merton from *Contemplation in a World of Action*: 'The world . . . is not a reality outside us for which we exist . . . It is a living and self-creating mystery of which I myself am a part, to which I am myself my own unique door. When I find the world in my own ground, it is impossible to be alienated by it.'

It is important then to look into ourselves: to purify our hearts – to look at our own bigotry honestly. If we are anti-war, anti-apartheid, anti-poverty, and anti-oppression; it is important to be ruthless in dealing with these forces in ourselves. In fact it is common knowledge that we tend to criticise the very things in life which reflect our worst selves. So have a look at violence in your thinking and speaking: examine your attitude to different races here in the U.K.; look at your giving to charity and your own attitude to food and drink; examine your behaviour towards those you live with and depend upon.

It is a special frustration of being older to experience the apparent antagonism of 'things'. We knock things over. We fall over a piece of furniture. We cannot easily control the way we eat or drink. It is just here that it is important to identify ourselves with the very things that frustrate. We must not despise the body as many anorexics do; nor must we neglect the mind as many newspaper readers do, nor must we ignore the spiritual as the worldly and un-churched tend to do. Life is a unity and we do best by coming to terms with its wholeness.

MEDITATION   **God Confronts**

Jesus replied, 'Anyone who loves me will heed what I say; then my Father will love him, and we will come to him and make our dwelling with him.'   John 14. 23

LENT 1

FIRST SUNDAY IN LENT

Jesus was in the wilderness forty days, tempted of Satan; and was with the wild beasts; and the angels ministered unto him.   *Mark 1.13*

COLLECT
Almighty God,
whose Son Jesus Christ fasted forty days in the
    wilderness,
and was tempted as we are, yet without sin:
give us grace to discipline ourselves
    in obedience to your Spirit;
and, as you know our weakness,
so may we know your power to save;
through Jesus Christ our Lord.

LENT 1   Monday   *Celebration*

Delia Smith's book of recipes, *Fun for One* has a lot of good ideas for those living alone. Unfortunately we don't all have the kind of kitchen that lends itself to exotic cookery; not quite the energy to take so much trouble just for ourselves. There is a lot to be said for having a celebration once in a while and what Delia calls 'enough for one', is very often quite enough for two as appetites are not always big when you get older, so why not invite your neighbour in to share 'the fun for one'. In the second half of this century the art of celebration has been re-discovered. It has always been basic in human life and never more so than when things are difficult. Take the opportunity when it comes your way.

Linked with the concept of celebration is enjoyment and delight and wonder. A recent film called *Witness*, made in Australia and directed by Peter Weir tells the story of a small boy of eight who by chance witnessed a savage attack which ended in murder. Later the boy was able to recognise the photograph of the man who did it and so bring to an end a long tale of corruption. The story line is a simple one, but the film was made remarkable because it was set amongst the Amish people of Pennsylvania in America where the Anabaptist simplicity of life persists and the people still possess a deep sense of wonder about the mystery of life and its value. The Amish society is brilliantly portrayed and the Christian standards clearly described. The total impact on the viewer is of sharing a glimpse of heaven. For me the several occasions in the film when grace was said communally at meals made an immediate impact. This was because the prayer was not forced or controlled but

14

quite spontaneous. These people were living close to God and wanted to celebrate this truth and live it out in their lives.

MEDITATION
The Anointing at Bethany

Jesus was at Bethany in the house of Simon the leper, when a woman approached him with a bottle of very costly perfume; and she began to put it over his head as he was at table. The disciples were indignant when they saw it . . . they said, 'It could have been sold for a large sum and the money given to the poor.' Jesus noticed, and said to them, 'Why make trouble for the woman? It is a fine thing she has done for me. You have the poor among you always, but you will not always have me. When she poured this perfume on my body, it was her way of preparing me for burial. Truly I tell you: wherever this gospel is proclaimed throughout the world, what she has done will be told as her memorial.' Matthew 26. 6–13

LENT 1 Tuesday *Cracking Up*

Whatever is meant by Paul's 'thorn in the flesh' he certainly saw it as an opportunity for spiritual training. 'To keep me from being unduly elated by the magnificence of such revelations, I was given a thorn in the flesh, a messenger of Satan sent to buffet me; this was to save me from being unduly elated.' (2 Cor. 12. 7) In our middle years it is not difficult to find many 'thorns in the flesh' to grumble about. Men are a good deal worse than women in this. It does not take much of a 'thorn' for the average male to see himself 'laid out on a cold slab':

women have a lot more sense and bolster themselves up by telling their friends and neighbours all about their latest symptoms and ills.

Psychologically we can find numerous small 'thorns' which annoy and make us feel low. Our eyes water, our legs ache, we don't seem to see or hear as well as we did and we don't sleep properly: we need a tonic or at least a talk with the doctor. That is how we feel. In fact it is probably the aftermath of 'flu or a bad cold: or it may be directly connected with the difficult business of not having a big enough 'say' in life. We draw attention by cossetting our smaller ills.

Of course a regular visit to the doctor is essential for check-ups. We must be ready to accept the advice given by our well meaning relations and friends, to the effect that we should get a hearing aid or a new pair of glasses! Perhaps the way through the small 'thorns' is to con-centrate on the main issue – our spiritual life.

We need to remember that God speaks all the time; in and after prayer, through conversation with friends, in Church services and through sermons and perhaps above all through a spiritual director. Nobody cracks up who takes his or her problems to God.

MEDITATION **The Good Shepherd**

The Lord is my shepherd;
I lack for nothing.
He makes me lie down in green pastures,
he leads me to water where I may rest;
he revives my spirit;
for his name's sake he guides me in the right paths.
Even were I to walk through a valley of deepest darkness

16

I should fear no harm, for you are with me;
your shepherd's staff and crook afford me comfort.

Psalm 23. 1–4

LENT 1 Wednesday
Through a glass darkly

Truth is, I believe, multi-sided like a sphere, the vision of God is hidden within it. The analogy of the darkness of space and the brightness of the stars sets a limitless range to revelation, God – Creator and Redeemer.

We long to see God; this is the endless quest of the soul: this is the Road to Jerusalem. So, in this piece we can try to catch a glimpse of God, in the darkness, and in the light. The former is more difficult to grasp because it is nearer ultimate reality. The Eastern Church has always had a grasp of this truth and for this reason has drawn many souls along the Road. At the same time the East has been slow to relate these insights which God has given, to the kind of day to day loving which Jesus taught his followers. We see this in their slowness to recognise the need for a whole ministry.

We learn the fundamental truths of God in the darkness. This is stated very clearly in the *Cloud of Unknowing* in the paragraph which occurs at the end of chapter 3. 'Reconcile yourself to wait in this darkness as long as is necessary, but still go on longing after him whom you love. For if you feel him or see him in this life, it must always be in this cloud, in this darkness. And if you work hard at what I tell you, I believe that through God's mercy you will achieve this very thing.'

It is for this reason that the soul needs spiritual counsel to interpret the darkness. Older Christians face a good deal of darkness in their lives. It comes from weakness, loneliness, and from the traumatic events of earlier days. We need not be afraid of this experience. Rather should we welcome it as an invitation to enter into the holy of holies where we simply 'wait upon God' in simple trust and expectation.

MEDITATION **Prayer in Darkness**

He himself withdrew from them about a stone's throw, knelt down and began to pray: 'Father, if it be your will, take this cup from me. Yet not my will but yours be done.'

Luke 22. 41

LENT 1 **Thursday** *The Vision of God*

When St Thomas was asked by Jesus to put his fingers into the holes that the nails had made and thrust his hand into the wound in his side, he was given that vision of God which we all long for if we are to cry out with him: 'My Lord and my God'. In a word our vision has to come through the familiar because that is how most of us see the Road to Jerusalem. There are not many natural mystics in the church or in the world, but there are lots of souls capable of seeing the vision of God in ordinary day to day events, provided always that we strive to catch the vision. This is what Jesus did for Thomas. Like so many, Thomas wanted proof when faith was really all he needed. Jesus was not unsympathetic. It was this common touch that gathered the crowds to hear him; this was the vision that brought together the five thousand to share in the miracle of the loaves and fishes. God believes in the ordinary person. We don't need special education, 'private schooling', 'selected intake', 'moneyed parents'; we need to learn to see God in art and science and in religion and humanity. Growing up is a fulfilment of God's gifts in us, the completion of ourselves; becoming what we truly are. All this is part of the vision of God. In his parables Jesus takes the ordinary event – the lost coin, the garden, the farm, the workers and their wages, the burglar, the army captain, weddings, illnesses, family life, as media for the vision of God. This is where God is always working; in ordinary events where he is speaking and we see him healing and teaching. We don't need to be clever. We simply need to be looking at him and wanting to give ourselves to him. Then, quite suddenly, perhaps when we are least expecting it he will say: 'Put your finger here ... Give me your hand, put it into my side.' What joy the vision of God brings.

MEDITATION **My Lord and my God**

Jesus came and stood among them, saying, 'Peace be with you!' Then he said to Thomas, 'Reach your finger here; look at my hands. Reach your hand here and put it into my side. Be unbelieving no longer, but believe.' Thomas said, 'My Lord and my God!' John 20. 26a–28

LENT 1   Frisday   *The Next Life*

Suppose we have married again: in the resurrection who belongs to whom, or have we got it wrong? This is the nub of the argument propounded by the Sadducees when they asked Jesus about the hypothetical case of the seven brothers, all of whom married the same widow in succession: in the resurrection whose wife shall she be? A good question you might say! The Sadducees, who did not believe in the resurrection, were the conservatives in the Jewish church, while the Pharisees (contrary perhaps to common belief) were the 'modernists' of their day who did believe. Jesus answers in the spirit of traditional Torah teaching: 'You are wrong, because you understand neither the scriptures nor the power of God. For at the resurrection men and women do not marry; no, they are like the angels in heaven'. He ends his statement by saying: 'God is God, not of the dead, but of the living.' There are several ideas of importance here. We tend to be so besotted with our life here on earth that we shut our eyes and ears to anything that suggests that this must come to an end at death. Nor are we too sure what is meant by the suggestion that we shall live 'like the angels': it sounds a bit mythical. Perhaps we would do better to approach the problem from the other end. God is God and human kind is his: he is the God of the living and it is our entry into a new life in God that matters. That is why I always like the analogy of the caterpillar, chrysalis and butterfly because it teaches the nature of resurrection life without attempting to define the structure. We shall be changed into his likeness from glory to glory.

So far as marriage partners are concerned, they matter

a great deal on earth because we need each other on this very human level, and we have the command to 'be fruitful and multiply'. The interesting thing about the analogy of the butterfly is that it takes up into the resurrection life, the whole of what came before, and transforms it. God is a spirit and we who worship him must worship him in spirit and in truth. This always suggests to me that in the next life we shall be one in spirit, and united in understanding and that all whom we have known intimately as well as socially will be closer to us and to each other than they were before.

We are called to exercise our faith and imagination and to be unselfish in our relationships with those whom we love most dearly and intimately. Jesus made only a few references to the 'next life' because I believe he wanted to stress the importance of living in the 'here and now' and making the very most of every opportunity that God gives for fullness, service and love.

MEDITATION **A Hymn of Triumph**

And when this perishable body has been clothed with the imperishable and our mortality has been clothed with immortality, then the saying of scripture will come true: 'Death is swallowed up; victory is won!' 1 Corinthians 15. 54

LENT 1 **Saturday** *Sitting on a Pillar*

Kenneth Leech in his magnum opus, *True God* (Sheldon Press 1985) talks about 'the desert fathers and their quest for God.' He mentions St Simeon Stylites

(390–459) the saint who sat on a pillar for many years seeking God and his own identity. 'The solitary life has continued to puzzle the Christian believers of later generations.' He quotes Phyllis McGinley's poem about St Simeon, and I do likewise, because it stresses both the extraordinary lengths to which Christian witness can go and the unconscious humour which so much of our Christianity evokes. At least it contains one message for senior citizens: 'be not afraid of doing something unusual if it is part of your personal belief and conscience.'

> On top of a pillar Simeon sat.
> He wore no mantle,
> He had no hat,
> But bare as a bird
> Sat night and day,
> And hardly a word
> Did Simeon say.
>
> Under the sun of a desert sky,
> He sat on a pillar
> Nine feet high.
> When Fool and his brother
> Came round to admire
> He raised it another
> Nine feet higher.
>
> The seasons circled about his head.
> He lived on water
> And crusts of bread
> (Or so one hears)
> From pilgrim's store
> For thirty years
> And a little more.

And why did Simeon sit like that,
Without a mantle,
Without a hat,
In a holy rage
For the world to see?
It puzzles me.
It puzzled many
A desert Father
And I think it puzzled the
Good Lord rather.

MEDITATION   **Patient Waiting**

*There was at that time in Jerusalem a man called Simeon.
This man was upright and devout, one who watched and
waited for the restoration of Israel, and the Holy Spirit was
upon him. It had been revealed to him by the Holy Spirit that
he would not see death until he had seen the Lord's Messiah.*
Luke 2. 25,26

LENT 2

SECOND SUNDAY IN LENT

To the Lord our God belong mercies and forgivenesses,
though we have rebelled against him.   *Daniel 9. 9*

COLLECT
Lord God Almighty,
grant your people grace
to withstand the temptations
    of the world, the flesh, and the devil,
and with pure hearts and minds
to follow you, the only God;
through Jesus Christ our Lord.

LENT 2   Monday   *Should I resign?*

When you return from a committee, having been unable
to follow a lot of the discussion because people mumble
instead of speaking clearly; having been frustrated by
the noise of the traffic outside, and consequently not
fully cognizant of what is being discussed, you wonder
whether the time has come to hand in your resignation.
Wisdom suggests discretion because it can be upsetting
if someone resigns apparently out of pique. Better perhaps to use the feeling of frustration as a signpost and
ask yourself whether it would be wise to set a date for
withdrawing.

Age does not always weaken faculties. Pope John 23
seemed to be able to command a very considerable
grasp of issues about which he felt deeply, and despite
his eighty years was able to set in motion Vatican II. On
the other hand most of us can recognise a weakness like
deafness, at least as far as committee work is concerned,
and this should be taken into consideration when we
hold on to jobs that could better be done by a younger
person. Of course we may have an expertise which is
unique in the work we have undertaken and here a
signpost of a different kind has to be sought – are we still
able to be useful? Self-assessment is very important.
Friends and well-wishers tend to flatter. They don't
want to upset us. Why not set a particular age like 75 or
80 as a datum line for decision making? Retirement at
65–70 is, in my opinion, a good thing because work can
still be done informally or as a hobby, and room is made
for those who are coming up to leadership and influence.

What about those of us who have bees in our bonnets? We tend to be both deaf and blind metaphorically to over-staying our time on a committee or in a piece of voluntary work. It is just here that rules are useful. There is nobody more difficult than the man or woman who has done a piece of work for fifty and more years and wants to continue to do it until death. The work inevitably suffers and younger aspirants do not get trained or given opportunity for experience. Bees in the bonnet are a sign of pride and pride is the deadliest of sins because it hinders life and growth. We sin very often when we press a personal quirk instead of seeing a wider issue. It is less easy as you get older to make a fair assessment of capability, so be self critical and do not give yourself the benefit of the doubt.

MEDITATION **Lord Open My Eyes**

'But happy are your eyes because they see, and your ears because they hear! Truly I tell you: many prophets and saints longed to see what you now see, yet never saw it; to hear what you hear, yet never heard it.' Matthew 13. 16,17

LENT 2 **Tuesday** *Gossip*

Gossip can be approached in two ways – positively or negatively. I incline to the former. I see gossip as a useful and positive activity – a human device to lessen tension and develop spiritual relaxation and renewal of interest in life. How many elderly ladies walk past our house up to the shops, just for the walk and in the hope of meeting someone with whom to have a word. Of course it all turns on what you mean by gossip as Dr C. E. M. Joad used to say on the Brains Trust radio programme during the war. Gossip can be a light-hearted exchange of news and views reasonably free from criticism but looked at negatively gossip can be malicious, 'catty' and dangerous to good relations. The salacious rumour that is passed on for the wicked pleasure it gives the teller: the confidence that has been shared by a friend and should not be spread further are clearly the working of evil and as such give gossip a bad name. Wisdom does not accrue to such people. We are wisely wary of them.

Is there then a guide line to be followed by those who wish to use the term gossip in a Christian way without simply refusing to play and taking up a 'holier than thou' attitude? I think there is.

We must cultivate a courageous and imaginative approach which does not pour scorn on what we hear, but immediately diffuses it with a remark that cancels out the danger. If we speak and think positively we can ask ourselves: 'Is it helpful or not?' If we share our news and views with attention on love we shall not go far wrong.

MEDITATION **Love is Kind**

And the tongue is a fire, representing in our body the whole wicked world. It pollutes our whole being, it sets the whole course of our existence alight, and its flames are fed by hell.
James 3. 6

LENT 2   Wednesday *The Wind of Change*

The English are supposed to be a very conservative nation, unwilling to make changes and inclined to stick to a familiar pattern of life and work. And yet our history suggests otherwise: Tudor political power is followed by industrial revolution, and this in turn gives birth to missionary enterprise, women's suffrage, children's charters, and the social services characteristic of the present century. Even in the somewhat eclipsed industrial life today we go on inventing and improving advanced technology.

It would be an interesting question to ask why it is that we tend to avoid the 'wind of change'. My own guess is that it is human nature to be slow to change and that we are not unique in this respect. There have always been 'luddites' and 'strikes' because of threatened redundancy, 'modern technology' and the fear of losing jobs. It is so much easier to carry on as you have always done and as your father did before you. In cases where a whole town is devoted to one industry the fears are doubled and trebled. The young and adventurous get out into a new area but the elderly, the weak, and the poor, are forced to remain. They become disgruntled, cynical, and depressed. What can be done?

God the Holy Spirit offers us the 'wind of change'. The disciples after the Resurrection suffered a good many of these depressing experiences but they were obedient to the Lord's command: 'Stay in the city then, until you are clothed with the power from on high'. This they did and the 'power of the Holy Spirit' was such that the gospel message was shared far and wide; miracles were per-

31

formed; the church of God grew and '. . . day by day the Lord added new converts to their number.' Acts 2. 47

MEDITATION **In Spirit and in Truth**

'But the time is coming, indeed it is already here, when true worshippers will worship the Father in spirit and in truth. These are the worshippers the Father wants. God is spirit, and those who worship him must worship in spirit and in truth.' John 4. 23,24

LENT 2   Thursday   *No No Nanette*

It is always nostalgic to have memories of past pleasures awakened after half a century has passed. Such was my experience when the Plymouth Theatre Royal production of the nineteen twenties musical *No No Nanette* visited Liverpool and played at the Empire Theatre to a first night audience of considerable age and enthusiasm. Many of us had seen the original touring company in the twenties and we could remember well the two most popular songs: 'Tea for Two' and 'I want to be Happy'. The absurd but simple story of a wealthy man who involved himself with three women and financed their respective interests, is relieved by a romance between Nanette and her boy friend. All very refreshing after recent decades of sex and violence. How loyal and adventurous the elderly often are when tempted by tickets at 'two for the price of one' on a Monday evening to give the show a rousing send-off. I felt very much at home watching twenties dance routines and the cloche hats. The sets were bright with art nouveau designs and the dresses matched. In the audience a guide dog was sitting dutifully by his master and crutches were prominent in several places. Grey hair was de rigueur and a good time had by all.

What does this add up to in terms of the spiritual life? Certainly two things emerge very clearly: the sheer enjoyment of nostalgia and the continuing pleasure of the theatre. In days when buses are filled with parties people can come into the city from neighbouring towns without too much hassle. The magic of the great proscenium arch remains throughout life. What pop groups and their music do for the young, and big bands like James Last's for the middle aged, the early musicals do for the senior citizen. Roll on Rose Marie and the Desert Song.

MEDITATION   **The Rainbow**

> *Look at the rainbow and praise its Maker;*
> *it shines with a surpassing beauty,*
> *spanning the heavens with its gleaming arc,*
> *a bow bent by the hands of the Most High.*
> Ecclesiasticus 43. 11, 12

LENT 2   Friday   *'Saint' John Lennon*

Although no one would call John Lennon a saint in the ordinary meaning of the word, he had a considerable following of admirers amongst the young. The service marking his death which Liverpool Cathedral organised was supported by thousands of young people and the

Dean made a moving tribute to Lennon's musical ability and his work for peace. By contrast a great many Liverpool people openly ignored the cathedral tribute and preferred to stay away in order to signify their disagreement with many of his views on drugs, sex, and race. Both groups were clearly right to express their strongly held views in tangible form: my wife and I found ourselves present at a kind of 'youth service' where the hymns and prayers echoed many of the Beatles lyrics. It is interesting to speculate what the young congregation felt. Certainly they were caught up in a very strong atmosphere and were glad they had come. Clearly too the Dean's words helped to formulate in many minds the un-spoken and deeply felt appreciation of John Lennon and to focus on his 'vision' of a world of fellowship, understanding and peace. They were prepared to relegate his 'failures' and his egotism to the background and to appreciate the kind of 'lead' which he attempted to give in the fratricidal world of today.

As we get older we become very conscious that our 'models' in life tend to come from areas of influence which we find attractive in music, art, religion, literature, poetry and so forth. If someone breaks the pattern we recognise, by designs that look bizarre, words that seem to be meaningless, and ideas which seem frankly absurd, then we look elsewhere. Many of the young have long ago given up hoping for inspiration for spiritual awareness from religious orthodoxies. But they are glad to be able to use a cathedral for a special 'statement' of their own belief. Is there a clue here to our understanding of faith today?

'And when I am lifted up from the earth I shall draw every-one to myself.'   John 12. 32

LENT 2   Saturday   *Favourite Psalm*

One of my earliest memories at my Grammar School was hearing Psalm 63 and falling in love with the spiritual yearning expressed so perfectly in the first nine verses. I specially like the 1662 Prayer Book translation of the psalm. Let me quote verses 1–9 for you:

O God, thou art my God: early will I seek thee.
My soul thirsteth for thee, my flesh also longeth after thee: in a barren and dry land where no water is.
Thus have I looked for thee in holiness: that I might behold thy power and glory.
For thy loving-kindness is better than the life itself: my lips shall praise thee.
As long as I live will I magnify thee on this manner: and lift up my hands in thy Name.
My soul shall be satisfied, even as it were with marrow and fatness: when my mouth praiseth thee with joyful lips.
Have I not remembered thee in my bed: and thought upon thee when I was waking?
Because thou hast been my helper: therefore under the shadow of thy wings will I rejoice.
My soul hangeth upon thee: thy right hand hath upholden me.

The Prayer Book translation is peculiarly apt and the use of the old English address to God absolutely right. A great sense of reverence is achieved and combined with a natural rhythm of song and prayer.

MEDITATION   **Rabbi Ben Ezra**

Grow old along with me!
*   The best is yet to be,*
The last of life, for which the first was made:
*   Our times are in his hand*
who saith 'A whole I planned,
*   Youth shows but half; trust God: see all, now be afraid!'*
                                        Robert Browning

LENT 3

THIRD SUNDAY IN LENT

The sacrifices of God are a broken spirit: a broken and
a contrite heart, O God, you will not despise.

Psalm 51. 17

COLLECT
Almighty God,
whose most dear Son went not up to joy
   but first he suffered pain,
and entered not into glory before he was crucified:
mercifully grant that we, walking in the way of the cross,
may find it none other than the way of life and peace;
through Jesus Christ our Lord.

LENT 3   Monday   *Violence*

August 6th was the date in 1945 when the atomic bomb
was dropped on Hiroshima in Japan. On any showing
this was a world shattering act of violence. Some com-
mentators saw it as 'the end of all wars': some saw it as
a speedy way of ending the Japanese war: some felt that
if life was to end suddenly then this was a quick way of
doing it – forgetting that those on the fringe of the
explosion suffered multiple injuries. Christians for the
most part saw it as the Judgment of God which indeed
it was. All nations have been trying to come to terms
with 'the bomb' ever since that date. Half a century has
passed. Disarmament has been debated and strong
nations have subscribed to treaty limitations of arms.
New ideas spring forth – including the United Nations.
The grim truth seems to be that until war is banned, as
slavery has now been banned in all civilized countries,
we stand on the brink of disasters of a dimension which
could completely eliminate life on our planet.

It is not for nothing that August 6th is kept in the Anglican Church calendar as the Feast of the Transfiguration.
The light of the glory of God shone forth in the face of
Jesus Christ and three chosen disciples were witnesses
of an event which is recorded in all three synoptic
gospels. The passion of Jesus is a continuous drama in
which he faces the full weight of evil, and finally death,
the ultimate sacrifice for humankind.

Violence breeds violence and we have seen an upsetting
resurgence of it in the second half of this century. Young
and old, we all need to take care today, to avoid confrontation with violence. It may well be forced upon us

as it was on Jesus but we are wise not to court disaster, unless, like Jesus we have a call to martyrdom.

MEDITATION   **The Epileptic Boy**

. . . a man came up to Jesus, fell on his knees before him, and said, 'Have pity, sir, on my son: he is epileptic and has bad fits; he keeps falling into the fire or into the water. I brought him to your disciples, but they could not cure him.' . . . Then Jesus spoke sternly to him; the demon left the boy, and from that moment he was cured.   Matthew 17. 14–18

LENT 3   Tuesday   *All Shall Be Well*

This famous and most comforting saying of Mother Julian of Norwich is something that we have all come to treasure more and more. So many things that we have done: so many things that have been done to us; and so many things that appear to have come 'at us' during our lives, seem to be 'unfair' as children say! When we look back the scene seems muddled and sometimes meaningless. Perhaps we are not very good at discerning the 'purpose of God in the life of the world'. In any case changing fashions and morals make it that much more difficult to judge. 'In our day things were very different' we say and imply criticism. But, says Dame Julian: 'All shall be well'.

I remember on an occasion sitting in a local train next to a young man got up in punk style, with multi-coloured hair that stood on end and a leather jacket bespattered with studs and badges: the effect was almost alarming, yet when he spoke he seemed a perfectly normal youth. When he moved off the train at his station he behaved like anyone else and I heaved a sigh of relief: there had not been a transistor radio blaring pop music; the only menace was the new style. So many of our lives have been lived with a kind of normality which we assume to be what everyone desires. Probably we have been living mainly amongst people who thought as we did. We have not had time to study the way-out types and the freaks. Life gave us what we wanted for the most part.

Dame Julian is reputed to have been an anchorite to whom travellers, enquirers, clergy, friends and the populace generally came to consult – a counsellor indeed! Her answers must have been full of wisdom because people continued to come, just as they came to the Curé d'Ars and to Tubby Clayton, the Toc H padre. Great preachers and counsellors have a quality that illuminates life 'on the way'. The enquirer goes away better able to see what to do, and how to do it.

MEDITATION   **God is Love**

My dear friends,
let us love one another, because the source
of love is God.
Everyone who loves is a child of God and knows God.

I John 4. 7

LENT 3 Wednesday *On Being Human*

Dorothy Sayers in her great work, *The Mind of the Maker*, bases her study of the Trinity on the concluding speech of St Michael in her play, *The Zeal of Thy House*. This is how it goes:

'For every work (*or act*) of creation is three fold, an earthly trinity to match the heavenly.

First (*not in time, but merely in order of enumeration*) there is the Creative Idea, passionless, timeless, beholding the whole work complete at once, the end in the beginning: and this is the image of the Father.

Second, there is the Creative Energy (*or Activity*) begotten of that idea, working in time from the beginning to the end, with sweat and passion, being incarnate in the bonds of matter: and this is the image of the Word.

Third, there is the Creative Power, the meaning of the work and its response in the lively soul: and this is the image of the indwelling Spirit.

An these three are one, each equally in itself the whole work, whereof none can exist without other: and this is the image of the Trinity.'

This I believe is the context of our humanity. Our delight in being human comes from this truth about God the Holy Trinity. I have loved being human myself and I have considered it many times as a wonderful gift from God. It is the experience of being, in the context of present, past, and future: the experience of love and pain in the context of family life and vocational calling; the experience of eternity in every conscious moment of time. We, in our humanity, know that life is precious and we feel that it should be meaningful and that in it we should find both ourselves and other people. This is the working of the Spirit teaching us the truth about God and ourselves. It is God who lifts us into the Godhead and enables us by the power of His Spirit to find our home there.

MEDITATION   **Life in Christ**

For to me life is Christ, and death is gain. If I am to go on living in the body there is fruitful work for me to do.

Philippians 1. 21,22

LENT 3   Thursday *Peace*

When we used the old Prayer Book and the long 'prayer for the whole state of Christ's Church' it was customary to preface this prayer with a few suggestions for special intercession, and very frequently there was a mention of prayer for peace. Perhaps it was the aftermath of war that caused this emphasis. I remember thinking about peace and realising that in reality it is a rare quality and one which most people define negatively as 'an absence of war'. Better really to pray for justice because justice lies behind genuine peace. Peace is a very inward thing associated with the quiet and sustained awareness of our vocation in the midst of activity and clamour. It is not a matter of escape from turmoil but maintaining calm within it. As someone once said to me: 'I try to make a space of silence round my soul'. So peace is something to be achieved by effort. It is also a gift from God. In it we can hope to meet God 'face to face'. As Studdert

Kennedy expressed it in his poem, *The Suffering God*:

> Peace does not mean the end of all our striving,
> Joy does not mean the drying of our tears;
> Peace is the power that comes to souls arriving
> Up to the light where God Himself appears

Peace is one of the mysteries of life: an experience of God which is greater than its earthly counterpart.

Let peace be your aim; that inward peace which closeness to God brings through prayer and which constitutes the springboard of power. Faith, hope, and love all come from this union with God. Peace is the power, as Studdert Kennedy says, 'that comes to souls arriving up to the light where God himself appears'.

MEDITATION   **The God of Peace**

Then the peace of God, which is beyond all understanding, will guard your hearts and your thoughts in Christ Jesus
Philippians 4. 7

LENT 3   Friday   *The Daffodils*

I wandered lonely as a cloud
    That floats on high o'er vales and hills,
When all at once I saw a crowd,
    A host, of golden daffodils,
Beside the lake, beneath the trees,
Fluttering and dancing in the breeze.

Continuous as the stars that shine
    and twinkle on the milky way,

They stretched in never-ending line
    Along the margin of a bay:
Ten thousand saw I at a glance
Tossing their heads in sprightly dance.

The waves beside them danced, but they
    Out-did the sparkling waves in glee:
A Poet could not but be gay
    In such a jocund company!
I gazed – and gazed – but little thought
What wealth the show to me had brought:

For oft, when on my couch I lie
    In vacant or in pensive mood,
They flash upon that inward eye
    Which is the bliss of solitude;
And then my heart with pleasure fills,
And dances with the daffodils.

                        W. Wordsworth

Sometimes profundity and simplicity are inextricably combined to make a work of genius like Wordsworth's *Daffodils*. A popular appeal usually has something to teach us about the basic needs of people in contemporary society. Liverpool can illustrate this truth. The city possesses several excellent parks, notably Sefton and Calderstones, but they have never been wholly successful with the masses. Victorian in concept they were placed where the rich and influential would walk, ride or drive, and view the trees and gardens. Today Sefton Park has been planted with thousands of daffodils – a prayer for cancer sufferers, and the crowds are returning and we can all share in this great joy. We can pray that our minds may be kept open to the popular and the good. That we may not be blind to planning events that will draw the many people and their children. That, like Wordsworth, we may see the glory of God in the world of today.

MEDITATION   **This Generation**

How can I describe this generation? They are like children sitting in the market-place and calling to each other,
We piped for you and you would not dance.
We lamented, and you would not mourn.
                                    Matthew. 11. 16,17

LENT 3   Saturday   *Did Paul see Jesus?*

Dr Coggan, the former Archbishop of Canterbury, asks this question in his book: *Paul: Portrait of a Revolutionary* (Hodder 1994). It seems likely that Paul and Jesus were more or less contemporary figures in history though the exact chronology is difficult to establish. Paul – or Saul as he was then called – came from a devout Jewish family and was brought up in the university city of Tarsus. No doubt he would have visited Jerusalem for the Passover on some occasions in his life even before he undertook serious study under Gamaliel. Dr Coggan asks: '. . . is it not possible, indeed highly likely, that the young teacher from Galilee and the young Pharisee from Tarsus would have looked into one another's eyes, and that Saul would have heard Jesus teach?' What a fantastic thought! If this was so could he have made the wrong choice on the first occasion and started his resistance to Jesus' teaching, only to face him all over again

47

in the blinding flash of insight on the Damascus Road? A fantastic idea, and what a challenge!

Most of us have fantastic ideas at times – we should look at these ideas and see whether we were right or wrong. It is never too late to meet Jesus on our particular Damascus Road. Human nature can be exceedingly obstinate. We persist in our own ideas despite clear 'proof' that we are wrong. We do not easily give up what we have held dear for a lifetime. In all this God is our helper. The Holy Spirit continues to inform and teach and illuminate and if we can allow a new honesty to fill our minds when the flash of insight is given, we can hope to see life new and whole once more.

MEDITATION   **Saul's Conversion**

He fell to the ground and heard a voice saying, 'Saul, Saul, why are you persecuting me?' 'Tell me, Lord,' he said, ' who you are.' The voice answered, 'I am Jesus, whom you are persecuting.' Acts 9. 4, 5.

LENT 4

FOURTH SUNDAY IN LENT

When Christ shall appear, we shall be like him; for we
shall see him as he is.   *I John 3. 2*

Almighty Father,
whose Son was revealed in majesty
    before he suffered death upon the cross:
give us faith to perceive his glory,
that we may be strengthened to suffer with him
and be changed into his likeness, from glory to glory;
who is alive and reigns with you and the Holy Spirit,
one God, now and for ever.

LENT 4   Monday   *Loneliness*

Many people are lonely. Our contemporaries die and
our ability to get about and see people lessens. We
become dependent on callers and visitors. Perhaps men
suffer even more than women in this respect: partly
because they are more interested in work and hobbies
and less concerned with talk round the parish pump.
Women have the great gift of genuine love for other
people and their appetite for news and gossip can be
redemptive. Two women talking together in the market
place can be priests to each other: simply because they
have a genuine concern and interest in the stories they
are recounting. Some will remember the famous
Belcher cartoon from *Punch*: 'You are a one, Mrs Jones';
'I 'as to be, Mrs Brown.' For men it is very often a
hobby, membership of a club, or some kind of handy-
work that helps.

Spiritually the solution to loneliness is intercessory
prayer. Already this has been mentioned a few times in
these notes. Why then do I stress it again? Quite simply
because when we pray for people we know who are in
need, or relations whom we only see rarely, or corre-
spondents with whom we have only occasional contact,
we are joining them in their lives 'in the spirit'. You
cannot be lonely if your quiet hour is concerned with
thinking about folk you know, people in need, and
relations whom you see only seldom. Our remembrance
of them illuminates our relationship.

Careful scrutiny of the TV and Radio programmes can
do wonders for lonely people. There is often a great deal
there on offer during the daytime period and consultation with relatives and friends can dig out fascinating

programmes which can easily be missed without this kind of help. Consult your friends and neighbours and make plans accordingly.

MEDITATION **The Value of Mission**

After this the Lord appointed a further seventy-two and sent them on ahead in pairs to every town and place he himself intended to visit. He said to them: 'The crop is heavy, but the labourers are few.' Luke 10. 1–2

LENT 4 Tuesday *My Patron Saint*

I don't think the average Anglican is altogether enthusiastic about saints: they seem to be stained glass window people a good deal separated from everyday life. An exception to this is to be found in Liverpool Cathedral where the Lady Chapel contains a number of windows commemorating some of the great Liverpool leaders like Kitty Wilkinson and Josephine Butler, while the new windows in the west-end bays commemorate such great figures as Wilson Carlile, William Temple, Charles Kingsley and Edward Elgar. There is much to be said for the cult of saints because human nature is naturally worshipful and someone to admire and copy draws out the best in us all. Some people have a favourite saint like Francis of Assisi, or Mother Julian of Norwich. The Church itself looks to Peter and Paul as founder saints and often the two men are linked in a single-remembrance as in The Alternative Service Book 1980. I was ordained on St Matthew's Day (September 21st) in 1933 and although we do not know much about

Matthew, his link with financial rectitude has been a useful inspiration when you have chosen a profession with modest monetary rewards and a family with many needs.

As we get older the church year can mean more. It provides a kind of structure which assists worship. We may not easily be able to enter fully into each festival as it comes round but we can feel the strong support which the church calendar gives. I have always liked the story of the monk who when asked what he did about his prayers when he was travelling about on preaching engagements replied that he 'leant back' on his community's prayers and felt completely protected and supported.

MEDITATION
The Choice of the Twelve

During this time he went out one day into the hill-country to pray, and spent the night in prayer to God. When day broke he called his disciples to him, and from among them he chose twelve and named them apostles: Simon, to whom he gave the name Peter, and Andrew his brother, James and John, Philip and Bartholomew, Matthew and Thomas, James son of Alphaeus, and Simon who was called the Zealot, Judas son of James, and Judas Iscariot who turned traitor.

Luke 6. 12–16

LENT 4 Wednesday *'Give Them a Break'*

Many of us in the older years have to be looked after and this involves all kinds of traumas both for the 'patient' and the 'nurse'. We are used to organising our own lives and we can become very selfish in this ploy. Other people do not have the time or the energy or even the sympathy to be at our beck and call. A sudden big change – a stroke, a fall, an accident, can totally change our whole way of life. From being able to do a lot of essential yet simple things on our own we suddenly become dependent upon someone else to do them for us. It is all too easy to resent this in a big way. We try to throw our weight about by becoming over-bearing, demanding, critical, miserable, cantankerous and plain selfish. Several lines of action are open to us. We can discover with the help of spouse, relatives, or friends, what things we can do safely for ourselves. This immediately reduces the wear and tear on those looking after us. We can try to be open to suggestions as to the way in which our new situation can be coped with by others: finance, location of a 'home',companionship, and our own special requirements, all of which have to be taken into consideration. Nothing can be a substitute for our own home. But a 'home' can be a place where we are looked after, and it can be a relief to our nearest and dearest. When we find ourselves in one of these 'homes' we can adjust to a routine of life which is more reminiscent of a hospital than a home. We accept the 'common round' that helps to make life worth while – sleep, toilet, meals, visitors, maybe a position on the balcony or in the garden where we can see and be seen. It is all a strain at first, but it can become a pattern into which we can fit and be reasonably happy.

Many elderly folk could emulate this and relax into the knowledge that the praying church is supporting them in their somewhat isolated existence. We are much more closely linked by a common human spirit than we often realise. Our human spirit is taken up into the Holy Spirit of God and we experience renewal.

MEDITATION   **The Visitation**

Soon afterwards Mary set out and hurried away to a town in the uplands of Judah. She went into Zechariah's house and greeted Elizabeth. And when Elizabeth heard Mary's greeting, the baby stirred in her womb. Then Elizabeth was filled with the Holy Spirit and exclaimed in a loud voice, 'God's blessing is on you above all women, and his blessing is on the fruit of your womb. Who am I, that the mother of my Lord should visit me? I tell you, when your greeting sounded in my ears, the baby in my womb leapt for joy. Happy is she who has had faith that the Lord's promise to her would be fulfilled!'   Luke 1. 39–45

LENT 4   Thursday   *'Speak Lord'*

A good many of us have said 'Speak Lord' and hoped for direction from God over some present or future action. One of the very aggravating things about the spiritual life is, quite simply, that we do not 'hear God speak' very often or very clearly. Perhaps we expect too much: something clear and dramatic! Elijah expected that on Mount Carmel, but the Lord spoke in a 'still small voice'. It behoves us therefore to be attentive rather than demanding, and expectant rather than bullying, in our approach to God. In a day like today when reverence is rare and 'fools rush in where angels fear to tread' we are more than wise to emulate Moses at the burning bush when he was told to remove his shoes because he stood on holy ground. A little more reverence and a little less noise would be more than welcome in the religious circles of today.

One clue about communication with God is that he does not necessarily 'speak English', or for that matter any other specific language. We do best when we revert to 'sign language': indicating by kneeling, looking or appealing, what it is we hope for. God knows the anguish and longing of our hearts. His answer to our unspoken prayer may well be hidden. We have to discern it in the events of the day as they occur. When the disciples were making their way to the 'upper room' where they were to prepare the passover supper they were told to follow a man carrying a pitcher of water: an unusual occurrence as women were the usual water carriers. This kind of observation and awareness serves the spiritually minded person well. It is possible to find one's way through a maze of problems and difficulties if we can discern the Lord's leading through simple observation.

MEDITATION   **Speak Lord**

The boy Samuel was in the Lord's service under Eli. In those days the word of the Lord was rarely heard, and there was no outpouring of vision. One night Eli, whose eyes were dim and his sight failing, was lying down in his usual place, while Samuel slept in the temple of the Lord where the Ark of God was. Before the lamp of God had gone out, the Lord called him, and Samuel answered, 'Here I am!' and ran to Eli saying, 'You called me: here I am.' 'No, I did not call you', said Eli; 'lie down again.' So he went and lay down. The Lord called Samuel again, and he got up and went to Eli. 'Here I am!' he said, 'Surely you called me.' 'I did not call, my son,' he answered, 'lie down again'. Samuel had not yet come to know the Lord, and the word of the Lord had not been disclosed to him. When the Lord called him for the third time, he again went to Eli and said, 'Here I am! You did call me.' Then Eli understood that it was the Lord calling the boy; he told Samuel to go and lie down and said, 'If someone calls once more, say, 'Speak, Lord; your servant is listening.' So Samuel went and lay down in his place.   I Samuel 3. 1–9

LENT 4   Friday   *Exercise*

Exercise as such is not mentioned in the Gospels though Paul refers to the 'games' in his letters. No doubt the brawny disciples – especially those who were fishermen, had plenty of exercise in the course of the daily and nightly work. Walking from village to village is mentioned in the gospel story and the mount of Transfiguration was climbed by Jesus and the three chosen disciples. There were no buses or trains in those days and wheeled vehicles would be ridden by charioteers and farmers. The donkey would be a familiar beast of burden. When a crowd assembled as in the case of the miracle of loaves and fishes it is not difficult to believe that many of those present would have brought a picnic meal with them. Life was energetic as it was for our own grandparents before the age of the motor-car. Today we tend to ride when we could walk, and take a taxi when it would do us good to find the railway station or the bus-stop. The motor car has its place today, in spite of the carnage each week from accidents: door to door for holidays and door to supermarket for the shopping and 'hopping round' to see friends at the weekend.

How important is exercise? Does it link up with prayer? I think it does. When we retire we are forever exhorted to take plenty of exercise. If we have a dog we take it out. Shopping is more interesting on foot when you can meet your friends. But what about the prayer walk or meditation? I have a good friend who has Parkinson's disease and can only walk slowly. On every fine day he walks the mile to his parish church and either sits inside to meditate if it is open, or outside on one of the seats if the weather permits. What a good idea.

MEDITATION   **The Games**

At the games, as you know, all the runners take part, though only one wins the prize. You also must run to win. Every athlete goes into strict training. They do it to win a fading garland; we, to win a garland that never fades. For my part, I am no aimless runner; I am not a boxer who beats the air. I do not spare my body, but bring it under strict control, for fear that after preaching to others I should find myself disqualified.

1 Corinthians 9. 24–27

LENT 4   Saturday   *Second Childhood*

The famous speech from Shakespeare's *As You Like It*: 'All the world's a stage and all the men and women merely players' ends with these words:

. . . Last scene of all,
That ends this strange eventful history,
Is second childishness and mere oblivion,
Sans teeth, sans eyes, sans taste, sans everything.'

Rather a caustic comment on old age and one which most of us hope will not apply in every respect to our own senior years. Thanks to scientific medicine, and social welfare, very efficient dentures and glasses, this eventuality is often circumvented and we have every reason to appreciate the help which our contemporary world supplies. One thing that does tend to become a bugbear as we get older is the return of childhood fears. This may be partly due to failing strength, or perhaps to our vocational gifts which made us sensitive in early days and consequently rather nervous about some people and situations which return to haunt our older years. Whereas in childhood we were unable to cope easily with fears because we were small and immature, now in old age we have behind us a life-time of experience. Fears may be inconvenient but they need not terrify. We have the means of grace to withstand them and make them subservient. In order to achieve this state of maturity it is necessary to look the fears 'straight in the face' and refuse to be bullied by them as we were in childhood. Experience dictates what we should do, and prayer enables us to carry it through. In this way the power of fears is undone and God is seen to triumph in our lives. This is the meaning of true sanctity. We live, but Christ lives within us and the 'saintly' person is one whose life is 'hid with Christ in God'. We do our work, whatever it is, with God's help and what people see in us is a maturity which God has filled with his Spirit, and which shines out as our true and real self.

MEDITATION **Humility**

'He was in the form of God; yet he laid no claim to equality with God, but made himself nothing, assuming the form of a

slave. Bearing the human likeness, sharing the human lot, he humbled himself, and was obedient, even to the point of death, death on a cross! Therefore God raised him to the heights and bestowed on him the name above all names, that at the name of Jesus every knee should bow – in heaven, on earth, and in the depths – and every tongue acclaim, "Jesus Christ is Lord", to the glory of God the Father.'

Philippians 2. 6–11

LENT 5
PASSION WEEK

FIFTH SUNDAY IN LENT: PASSION SUNDAY

Jesus died for all, so that they which live should live no longer for themselves, but unto him who died and was raised to life for them.   *2 Corinthians 5. 15 (adapted)*

COLLECT
Most merciful God,
who by the death and resurrection of your Son Jesus
    Christ
delivered and saved mankind:
grant that by faith in him who suffered on the cross,
we may triumph in the power of his victory;
through Jesus Christ our Lord.

LENT 5   Monday in Passion Week
Self-examination

Old age is rather like childhood in reverse. As children we are limited by age, size, and lack of experience: elderlies are limited by advanced years, various physical and mental handicaps, and too much experience – we have seen it all before! But, not to worry, the experience we have had, no-one can take away from us. It is very useful. It teaches us to be careful and put our hands on the banisters when we descend the stairs. It teaches patience because we used to be able to do it twice as fast as we can now. It teaches us that it is better not to complain because if we do, people will write us off as bores. It is not easy. Very few, except our own contemporaries, are at all sympathetic. People smile benignly and think, 'there he/she goes again.' It is very humiliating and as for our prayers, well, they can be a dead loss. We are tempted to give them up. So what should we do?

I am always rather cheered by the amusing, even humiliating, story of Zacchaeus in Luke 19. Not that he was elderly. He must have been pretty agile to be able to climb into the sycamore tree. He apparently had a great curiosity and he wanted to catch a glimpse of Jesus without being spotted. He was also self-aware: he knew that his job made him unpopular. But he persisted and he was rewarded. 'Today I want to stay at your house.' What a surprise! Down he comes and back home with the Master he goes: lots of things no doubt buzzing round in his mind: 'Good heavens, what am I going to say about my kind of "pulling a fast one"? It will be useless to cover-up: Jesus will see through me easily enough. I can sense that. I may as well come clean and tell the whole sordid story. At least he doesn't appear to hate me.' And that was how it worked out.

A bit of rapid self-examination on the way to supper, and then afterwards in the relaxed atmosphere of the evening a 'heart to heart' and the chance to put things right. Most of us are not very spectacular in our mis-doings. We tend to be touchy, a bit mean, and anxious to be noticed: we have our ways of ministering to our own desires and we get very critical of people and things. We could learn a lot from Zacchaeus.

MEDITATION **The Blessing of Work**

Jesus saith: wheresoever there are two, they are not without God, and where there is one alone, I say: I am with him.
  'Lift up the stone,
  and there you shall find me,
  cleave the wood,
  and I am there.'
from the Oxyrhynchus Papyrus,
discovered in 1897 in Egypt

LENT 5   Tuesday in Passion Week
Arrow Prayer

When concentration becomes less easy it is often a good idea to pray 'as you go'. Gone are the days when people toiled through long lists of names. The chief use of lists in the older years is to provide an aide memoire for God-children, the hospitalised for whom prayer has been requested, and particular groups we are connected with. Practise arrow prayer.

I have a half-hour bus ride into the centre of Liverpool from Aigburth and can use this time for lifting up to God the various people visible from the bus, old and young, trying to guess what their work might be, and discerning if possible special needs arising out of poverty, handicaps, or difficult and unusual work. Then there are the vehicle drivers – buses, taxis and cars, and the people shopping. If it is early in the day children are about, and the milkman, the postman, the lollipop lady and the police. They all need a prayer rather than criticism. There are many occasions when senior citizens come up against problems – cycles on the footpath, general rudeness and inconsiderateness – and it is all too easy to become grumblers. Perhaps there is a hidden regret that we are no longer able to get about so easily as we did. Nevertheless we do best by maintaining patience and courtesy with a smile.

Arrow prayer offsets criticism very effectively. We turn a grumble into a positive desire that all may be well with the person concerned. A couple in love call for a prayer that marriage, if it comes along, may be successful, happy and lasting. The woman expecting a baby needs a prayer that all may go well with the birth and that the child will have good parents and a happy home. The severely handicapped need support in coming to terms with themselves and their problems: the out of work youth needs understanding, purpose, and hope. We also see a lot of people who are very fit, and we can thank God for them and pray that we may be equally fortunate.

Jesus prays for us

That is why he is able to save completely those who approach God through him, since he is always alive to plead on their behalf.   Hebrews 7. 25

LENT 5   Wednesday in Passion Week
Besetting Sins

I associate the words besetting sins with my confirmation classes of sixty years ago. I never quite understood what the two words meant at the time because they were not in my own vocabulary. Nowadays I doubt if the two words together are in anyone's vocabulary. I can't remember hearing them used at all in church circles during the past half-century. When I look back on those early days I realise that I was only vaguely conscious of the main sources of my sins. In the older years this is much easier, though not always palatable. We have been living with ourselves for long enough to know the 'attack' of pride, lust, envy, anger and the rest pretty well. The problem is how to cope when will-power seems weak, prayer sporadic, and consciousness of God often absent. One factor in our favour is the self-knowledge which over the years – especially if we have maintained some prayer – will have become familiar. The words besetting sin can take on a new life and make us properly aware of the dangers of persistent selfishness. We learn to differentiate between demanding comfort and attention and being ready to fit in with the household or institution.

The old enemies are there – the world, the flesh and the devil. Self-examination should proceed along familiar lines. We ask ourselves in what way we love self more than God in body, mind, will and soul? Though seniors, we are still servants – servants of God, and it remains important to take precautions against the old familiar temptations. Lord, open our eyes that we may see ourselves not only as others see us but as you see us. In this way we should be able to deal with our besetting sins and make our confession in this Passion Week.

MEDITATION **Think on These Things**

And now, my friends, all that is true, all that is noble, all that is just and pure, all that is lovable and attractive, whatever is excellent and admirable – fill your thoughts with these things.
Philippians 4. 8

LENT 5   Thursday in Passion Week
Vocation

There are three callings which in the eyes of the world are not exactly recognised for the importance to the community which in my opinion they hold: the Publican, the Lengthsman, and the Lavatory Attendant. Highest in general esteem would be the publican who has a difficult job in that he has to satisfy the customers while maintaining sobriety and order: he must protect the staff, and balance the books, showing at all times a bonhomie which makes the publican a kind of 'vicar'. All honour to such men and women for they must surely rank high in the eyes of God. The person who keeps the street clean has a unique opportunity today for this operation in our contemporary world which considers it a 'right' to drop the can/carton/bag so that the cleaner may pick it up! No thought for the hundreds of people who walk up and down the road looking at the filthy litter until such time as the official cleaner arrives with brush and trolley. What a difference it made to the success of the International Garden Festival in Liverpool that a whole team of cleaners were constantly working to keep the place tidy. It was always a pleasure to be there. As for the lavatory attendant, I have always liked the story of the man whose vocation in life was to become head cleaner in a large public lavatory. He achieved this ambition and fulfilled his vocation by making the place sparkle, with all the brass shining and everybody welcomed with a smile. Such men and women cannot be far from the Kingdom of Heaven.

There are many jobs in life that are essential for the welfare and happiness of the community and the three I have cited are amongst them. Other jobs are self-evidently valuable: food producers, home builders, makers of furniture, teachers, youth leaders, and sports instructors, clergy and ministers. We should value these vocations highly because they meet basic needs in humankind.

MEDITATION   **The Crown of Life**

The church member in humble circumstances does well to take pride in being exalted; the wealthy member must find his pride in being brought low . . .   James 1. 9.
Happy is the man who stands up to trial! Having passed that test he will receive in reward the life which God has promised to those who love him.   James 1. 12.

LENT 5   Friday in Passion Week
Rule of Life

In the older years a rule of life comes into its own. Not just the obedience, but because a Christian 'way of life' has become familiar. All those who have taken prayer seriously during the main section of their working lives, find that in retirement it still makes demands upon the day. Giving God time has become such a habit that to omit it is to damage oneself. But here again it is not a slavish obedience to an exact time, nor to an exact moment, nor is it necessarily the continuance of a pattern established in the middle years. It is simpler than that: it is making time for God as one makes time for meals, for sleep, and for chores. In my own case, being an early riser I was always in the habit of keeping an hour before breakfast for prayer: usually office or Eucharist, Bible reading, meditation and intercession; now I do this after breakfast, but still putting it first. It is good to plan a rhythm of work for the morning on most days and then take time for relaxation, rest, visiting and so forth later in the day. Morning work would include the chores, letters, cooking, cleaning, difficult reading and the fulfilment of obligations.

Dr Somerset Ward used to say that after seventy a rule of life ceased to be an obligation. There is great wisdom in learning to relax a rule, and not become obsessionally dominated by it. The principle of prayer, rest and work, in that order, remains an important truth for the average activist English man or woman. This way we cease to be such a nuisance to other people because we have got our priorities right.

Sundays will naturally include Holy Communion and hearing a sermon when these are normally possible. In retirement, there is no obligation to attend a big and perhaps 'noisy' service where lots of children are milling about, not is it important to be in church more than once on a Sunday. We need to have a plan and if we are in need of transport, it can usually be provided.

MEDITATION **Wisdom**

> *Put all your trust in the Lord and do not*
> *rely on your own understanding.*
> *At every step you take keep him in mind,*
> *and he will direct your path.*
>
> Proverbs 3. 5,6

LENT 5 Saturday in Passion Week
Writing to the Paper

One of the direct results of retirement is a sense of our lessening influence in affairs. So we say, when we feel this sense of frustration: 'I will write to the papers'. And very often we do just this and the letter tends to read more like a complaint than a strong statement. The simple answer is, 'Don't write to the papers', but this is not always wise because, even in retirement many people are still known to be experts in certain areas of study and expertise, which means that their comment can be both relevant and needed. On the other hand the papers are full of letters from disgruntled men and women who are more concerned to make their own particular point than supplying or correcting information. So what do we do? Perhaps the solution lies in limiting our output to matters on which we have some knowledge as well as strong views.

For myself I stick to the work that has occupied me throughout a half-century of ministry, namely prayer and the spiritual life, adding to this one or two subjects which have been life-long interests like a 'whole ministry' of men and women, and an enlightened sexual education for children and young people in home, school and society.

I have also joined the Howard League for Prison Reform because I consider that prison sentences are too long and that prison for most crimes is nowadays an irrelevance.

Writing to the Home Office against the imprisonment of Sarah Tisdall for an offence against the Official Secrets Act, drew forth a reply a month or two later. This at least was gratifying. One has a sense of making a contribution towards better justice.

The whole scene is not without its hopefulness provided we don't dissipate our energies, or become cynical. Decisions about writing to the papers, or otherwise attempting to exercise influence, should be made in the context of faith and prayer. We live in an age of specialisation and our word is listened to much more willingly if we are known to be knowledgeable on the subject.

MEDITATION   **Writing Letters**

I add this greeting in my own hand – Paul. Remember I am in prison. Grace be with you.   Colossians 4. 18

LENT 6
HOLY WEEK

SIXTH SUNDAY IN LENT: PALM SUNDAY

Hosanna to the Son of David: Blessed is he who comes
in the name of the Lord; Hosanna in the highest!

Matthew 21. 9

COLLECT
Almighty and everlasting God,
who in your tender love towards mankind
    sent your son our Saviour Jesus Christ
to take upon him our flesh
and to suffer death upon the cross:
grant that we may follow the example
    of his patience and humility,
and also be made partakers of his resurrection;
through Jesus Christ our Lord.

LENT 6 Monday in Holy Week
Prayer in Pain

In November 1984 Rosamund Essex, a former Editor of the *Church Times*, wrote a piece for that paper on 'prayer in the midst of pain'. A good deal of what she said in that article is appropriate to the condition of old age. 'Prayer in pain is largely an act of the will. You *wish* you could pray. That is the prayer.' We wish we could concentrate. We would like to have a system but it eludes us. Instead we could do worse than adopt Miss Essex's plan which was to offer her inability. 'I give you this difficult time for – battered children, prisoners of conscience, victims of war, the lonely, the bereaved, the criminal.' She ends her article with a quotation from Brother Lawrence: 'I wish you could convince yourself that God is often nearer to us, and more effectively present with us, in sickness than in health.'

Good Christian people tend to think that in times of pain and sickness it will be easier to pray because this is what Jesus did when faced with the cross in the Garden of Gethsemane. Many of us have been taught that illness can be a time when we should turn to God for his help very specifically. When we are actually suffering pain, in hospital, or at home, prayer seems quite impossible. Let us accept this and be content with fleeting thoughts and aspirations, arrow prayers for help and strength, and recollections of how Jesus prayed under such circumstances.

A very good way to encourage ourselves and build confidence in God in the face of illness and pain, is to request the prayers of our visitors and friends. When we

LENT 6 Wednesday in Holy Week
'Brace Yourself'

A particular hazard of the older years is the devastating effect that a bad cold or influenza can have upon the whole bodily system. It takes time to recover from a bad bout and very often the process of recovery re-sensitises old complaints. Our legs ache; we puff and blow; we grumble and we are altogether very sorry for ourselves and we let everybody know.

There are a few well tried ways of breaking up this syndrome of self-pity. The first is 'take your time'. Be patient with yourself and be grateful for an enforced 'confinement to barracks'. If you can 'medicate yourself' all well and good and don't be afraid to take twice as long as usual. The second rule is to be interested in other people, at home, while shopping, at church, and in the club. Nothing so quickly disperses gloom and self-pity as a genuine concern for others. Listen to their complaints and you will feel better in no time! The third rule is to offer your unpleasant experiences to God in arrow prayer. Instead of cursing yourself and everybody else, try asking the Lord to use the occasion.

It is always salutary to remember that one of the reasons why children like their grandparents is that there is always time. Children like to be in the centre of what is going on, and round the kitchen table or getting off to school are not occasions when parents can spare much time to 'stop, look, and listen'. But the elderly very often can. Be grateful for your enforced leisure and your slowing down. Put it to good use. Say, whenever you get the opportunity: 'Lord use me now', and when you have done your bit of listening and sympathising, end your prayer with, 'Thank you Lord for using me'.

MEDITATION   **A Useful Lunch**

Looking up and seeing a large crowd coming towards him, Jesus said to Philip, 'Where are we to buy bread to feed these people?' He said this to test him; Jesus himself knew what he meant to do. Philip replied, 'We would need two hundred denarii to buy enough bread for each of them to have a little.' One of his disciples, Andrew, the brother of Simon Peter, said to him, 'There is a boy here who has five barley loaves and two fish; but what is that among so many?' Jesus said, 'Make the people sit down.' There was plenty of grass there, so the men sat down, about five thousand of them. Then Jesus took the loaves, gave thanks, and distributed them to the people as they sat there. He did the same with the fish, and they had as much as they wanted.   John 6. 5–11

LENT 6   Maundy Thursday
Corpus Christi

If we have been keen church people all our lives the likelihood is that we shall keep our keenness into the older years. Are there dangers in this stance? If we are black and white types – meaning that we see things wholly right or wrong, then we tend to be even more obstinate in old age than when we were young. We call it 'holding firmly to our faith'. In cases where people have been rather woolly in their faith, they tend to become more so in the older years. In truth, age and experience should make it more possible to see things whole: to understand another point of view more easily. Anglicans specially have this opportunity because there have always been 'high, low, and broad' church people. So, amongst other things, Lent offers a special opportunity to listen attentively to the viewpoints of those with whom we disagree.

A very good way of doing this in Holy Week is to worship on Maundy Thursday, when the Holy Communion was instituted by Jesus in the 'Upper Room'. In the Middle Ages another feast was inaugurated on the Thursday after Trinity Sunday – called Corpus Christi – The Body of Christ – when similar thanksgivings were made for the institution of the Eucharist. Historically Maundy Thursday has more of the character of a memorial, while Corpus Christi tends to emphasise thanksgiving. Both are needed in today's Church. We do well when we can discern the teaching given by Jesus both from the standpoint of sacrifice and also of thanksgiving.

MEDITATION
The Elizabethan Quatrain

Christ's was the word,
Who spake it,
And what that word doth make it
That I believe and take it.

LENT 6 Good Friday   *The Cross*

Good Friday is the saddest and most solemn day in the Church year. For about 25 years it was my custom to offer the Three Hours Devotion on Good Friday, from 12 noon to 3 p.m. in some church in the diocese where it was observed. I remember on one particular Good Friday that I drove my Land Rover from Coniston Cold in the middle of the Yorkshire Dales to Sedbergh in the north; a distance of some twenty-five miles through country lanes. The occasion was memorable for me because I met Bill Long for the first time and we became life-long friends. At that time he was teaching French at Sedbergh School and functioning as a Reader in Sedbergh Parish Church. Our meeting began a friendship which continues unabated today. Forty years on Bill is now a priest in the Anglican Church and continues to serve in Sedbergh parish as he has done all his life.

Good Friday is a holy day. Jesus consummates his life and work and seals it with his death on the Cross at the hands of the Romans and by the betrayal of us all. By his death and resurrection Jesus Christ redeems the world.

> There was no other good enough,
>   To pay the price of sin;
> He only could unlock the gate
>   of Heaven, and let us in.

'God was in Christ reconciling the world to himself.' (2 Corinthians 5.19). 'And when I am lifted up from the earth I shall draw everyone to myself.' (John 12.32) 'It was by the name of Jesus Christ of Nazareth, whom you crucified, and whom God raised from the dead; through him this man stands here before you fit and well.' (Acts 4. 10)

MEDITATION

> *the sun will be darkened,*
> *the moon will not give her light;*
> *the stars will fall from the sky,*
> *the celestial powers will be shaken.*
>> Matthew 24.29

LENT 6   Saturday in Holy Week
Easter Eve

Easter Eve or Holy Saturday should be a quiet day after the trauma of Good Friday. The disciples are stunned and can only wait and wonder. The women busy themselves with the preparations for the burial and the anointing. This way they overcome to some extent the feeling of anxiety and sadness. Holy Saturday in the Anglican Church today is usually occupied with the preparations for Easter Day. Decorating, lights, polishing and clean linen for altar and choir: women find this a healing and hopeful occupation while the men tend to hide like the disciples.

The first light of dawn will herald the Easter proclamation. He is Risen, Alleluia. He is risen indeed. We all look forward to shouting this acclamation of praise and glory on Easter Day.

MEDITATION

Joseph took the body, wrapped it in a clean linen sheet, and laid it in his own unused tomb, which he had cut out of the rock. He then rolled a large stone against the entrance, and went away. Matthew 27. 59,60

EASTER

EASTER DAY

On the first day of the week the disciples went to the tomb, and they found the stone rolled away from the tomb. Alleluia!   *Luke 24.1 (adapted)*

COLLECT
Lord of all life and power,
who through the mighty resurrection of your Son
overcame the old order of sin and death
to make all things new in him:
grant that we, being dead to sin
and alive to you in Jesus Christ,
may reign with him in glory;
to whom with you and the Holy Spirit
be praise and honour, glory and might,
now and in all eternity.

MONDAY IN EASTER WEEK
The Emmaus Experience

It has always astonished me that keen and intelligent Christians should be so surprised when questions are raised about the central truths of our Faith – Incarnation, Resurrection, Ascension and Pentecost. The growth and life of the Church turns on thinking about God and his purpose in these mysteries. Any attempt to define them in human language is bound to be limited by the nature of language itself. Take the splendid phrase from the Nicene creed: God from God, Light from Light, with capitals to emphasis the God-ness of the description. This is simply a poetic attempt to describe the Person of Christ. We can never define God, though we shall rightly go on trying to do so. And in the process we shall disagree with each other about what is meant by the words we use, and we shall tend to get upset as we are misunderstood in turn. Historically when disagreement reached large proportions we set up tribunals, star chambers, crusades and inquisitions and started persecuting one another. What we really need is to see Jesus crucified, dead and buried and we need the Emmaus Experience. Religion is a funny business. We see conflict between different faiths: Jews, Christians, Muslims, Sikhs, Buddhists, Hindus – all fearing each other instead of listening to each other. It is just the same with churchmanship, there are high, low, and middle attitudes in all faiths and creeds. So, what do we do? We need humility and love. We need to learn what it all means from the Risen Lord. He is the Emmaus Experience. We need to meditate on it daily.

The Risen Lord

By this time they had reached the village to which they were going, and he made as if to continue his journey. But they pressed him: 'Stay with us, for evening approaches, and the day is almost over.' So he went in to stay with them. And when he sat down with them at table, he took bread and said the blessing; he broke the bread, and offered it to them. Then their eyes were opened, and they recognized him; but he vanished from their sight. They said to one another, 'Were not our hearts on fire as he talked with us on the road and explained the scriptures to us?' Luke 24. 28–32

TUESDAY IN EASTER WEEK
The Great Forty Days

Traditionally 'the great forty days' between Easter and Whitsun have been associated with the prayer of expectancy – waiting for the coming of the Holy Spirit. In our older years a very good way of observing these days is to lay emphasis on intercession. Praying for other people is an exercise in self-denial and waiting.

We could begin with remembrance of our own family. Relatives are often numerous when we reach middle age. There are grandchildren, great nieces and nephews as well as siblings and their families: many of whom depend upon us for the letter, the telephone call, or the visit we could organise; we may have a considerable commitment of care and concern. Travel can be difficult and writing letters is sometimes a chore that we don't easily face except at Christmas time. It all points to the value of intercessory prayer which can be like the loving inspection of the family albums, or a glance through our birthday book each month. Perhaps we can develop a plan to help those who depend upon us for encouragement and support.

The Holy Spirit caught up the nervous disciples and apostles in Jerusalem on the day of Pentecost. The waiting disciples were filled with grace and power and went out to witness and heal. The Church had started and all those waiting were drawn in. So we pray to God that the Holy Spirit will support, heal, and sanctify the Christian family launching us out into a world of great human need.

MEDITATION   **The Spirit of God**

In the last days, says God, I will pour out my Spirit on all mankind; and your sons and daughters shall prophesy; your young men shall see visions, and your old men shall dream dreams.   Acts 2.17

WEDNESDAY IN EASTER WEEK
Spiritual Growth

Most of us have young relatives and we enjoy it when they come to see us. Perhaps we were privileged to introduce them to the circus or the theatre for the first time when their parents were busy. It is possible for the elderly to have an excellent relationship with the younger generation, a relationship that pays dividends because of the stimulus that youth brings.

I have very happy memories myself of my 'favourite aunts', my mother's sisters, who were still young enough to enter into games and parties at Christmas time. I have often compared someone very favourably by saying 'she is just like my favourite aunt'. Our nephews and nieces have cultivated us in their younger days because of our enthusiasm. Now in old age we return the compliment by getting to know them better and taking a much needed interest in their lives.

Relations and friends are not to be despised. They can be of great comfort in old age. Jesus collected his first disciples from such a group who made their living in the vicinity of the Sea of Galilee. We do well to cultivate our relations and friends. Life turns on relationships with God and with people. Church life is, or should be, as St Paul suggested, life 'hid with Christ in God'.

This way growth takes place and daily life becomes a resurrection life, in which we find a two-way relationship between youth and age and a spiritual growth that develops from the fullness of life in the Risen Lord.

MEDITATION
New Life in the Risen Lord

Praised be the God and Father of our Lord Jesus Christ! In his great mercy by the resurrection of Jesus Christ from the dead, he gave us new birth into a living hope, the hope of an inheritance, reserved in heaven for you, which nothing can destroy or spoil or wither. Because you put your faith in God, you are under the protection of his power until the salvation now in readiness is revealed at the end of time.

I Peter 1.3–5

Index of Bible References